WORLD CONSTITUTION

CONSTITUTION FOR THE UNITED
FEDERATION OF THE WORLD

First published by O-Books, 2018
O-Books is an imprint of John Hunt Publishing Ltd., No. 3 East St., Alresford, Hampshire SO24 9EE, UK
office1@jhpbooks.net
www.johnhuntpublishing.com

For distributor details and how to order please visit the 'Ordering' section on our website.

Text copyright: Nicholas Hagger 2017

ISBN: 978 1 84694 991 3
978 1 78099 662 2 (ebook)
Library of Congress Control Number: 2017957734

A CIP catalogue record for this book is available from the British Library.

Design: Stuart Davies

Printed and bound by CPI Group (UK) Ltd, Croydon, CR0 4YY, UK

We operate a distinctive and ethical publishing philosophy in all areas of
our business, from our global network of authors to production and
worldwide distribution.

Selected Stories: Follies and Vices of the Modern Elizabethan Age
Selected Poems: Quest for the One
The Dream of Europa
Life Cycle and Other New Poems 2006 – 2016
The First Dazzling Chill of Winter
The Secret American Destiny
Peace for our Time
World State

"Unless we establish some form of world government, it will not be possible for us to avert a World War III in the future."

Winston Churchill, 1945

"Human society can be saved only by Universalism."

Emery Reves, *The Anatomy of Peace*, 1945

"Mankind can be saved only if a supranational system, based on law, is created to eliminate the methods of brute force."

Albert Einstein, 1950

"History is now choosing the founders of the World Federation. Any person who can be among that number and fails to do so has lost the noblest opportunity of a lifetime."

Carl van Doren

CONTENTS

Note on Provenance   ix

Preface on Constitutions   xi

Constitution for the United Federation of the World   1

Preamble   3

Chapter I: Purposes and Principles

      Articles 1–2   3

Chapter II: Membership

      Articles 3–6   5

Chapter III: Structure

      Articles 7–16   6

Chapter IV: The Inter-national Level

      Articles 17–26   10

Chapter V: The Supranational Level

      Articles 27–45   13

Chapter VI: Peace Dividend

      Articles 46–51   23

Chapter VII: Rights and Freedoms

      Articles 52–86   26

Chapter VIII: Equal Rights and Justice

      Articles 87–101   34

Chapter IX: World Citizens' Rights

      Articles 102–119   38

Chapter X: Protection of Rights and Freedoms

      Articles 120–130   43

Chapter XI: Emblem, Flag, Anthem and Location

      Articles 131–134   45

Chapter XII: Supremacy of Constitution

      Articles 135–136   47

Chapter XIII: Amendments

      Articles 137–139   47

Chapter XIV: Signing and Ratification

      Articles 140–145   48

Appendices

    Precedents and data on which the Constitution is based   53
    1. 26 Constitutional Precedents and 204 Constitutions   55
    2. World Parliamentary Assembly, Allocation of
        850 Seats   69
    3. World Commission, Allocation of 27 Seats   73
    4. World Senate, Allocation of 92 Seats   75
    5. Diagram/Flow Chart of the Supranational
        Authority: The Structure of the World State   77
    6. Chart of 25 Civilizations and Cultures from
        One to One   78

Sources for Articles in the Constitution for the United
    Federation of the World   81

Bibliography   87

Note on Provenance

Nicholas Hagger based this 145-Article Constitution for the United Federation of the World (UF) on the ideas in his works, in particular *The World Government* and *World State* (an introduction to the UF); and on the precedents listed in Appendix 1. For further details, see the Preface, p.xi and Sources for Articles in the Constitution for the United Federation of the World (pp.81–85), which relates the Articles to precedents. For background, see his work *Peace for our Time*.

This Constitution was assembled (on and off while preparing *World State*) between 25 August and 11 October 2017.

Preface on Constitutions

Definition of 'constitution'

A constitution is "the mode in which a state is constituted or organised", "the system or body of fundamental principles according to which a nation, state or body politic is constituted and governed" (*Shorter Oxford English Dictionary*). It is "the body of fundamental principles or established precedents according to which a State or other organisation is acknowledged to be governed" (*Concise Oxford Dictionary*). A good constitution has clarity, sense and succinctness, and inspires and resonates.

Written constitutions dictate the rules that are to govern societies. The American constitution was agreed after a Constitutional Convention in Philadelphia involving 55 delegates and lasting 116 days (25 May–17 September) that brought in the Federal Constitution in 1787.

Number of past constitutions and precedents

A total of 158 sovereign nation-states now have written constitutions, as do 9 partially-recognised countries and 13 dependent territories, and there are 6 uncodified constitutions and 18 constitutions of former countries, making a total of 204 constitutions (see Appendix 1). The UN has a Charter and the Universal Declaration of Human Rights, NATO has a Treaty and the EU has a succession of Treaties that include the Paris, Rome, Maastricht, Amsterdam, Nice and Lisbon Treaties. It also has the European Convention on Human Rights and the Charter of Fundamental Rights of the European Union. There are 26 constitutional precedents (see Appendix 1A). The UK does not have a written constitution, and this may be one of the reasons for Brexit: the British do not like to be tied down to the written rules of the EU.

Since the establishing of the UN there have been two flawed attempts at writing constitutions with the intention of founding a new World State. Neither seeks to replace the UN. The Constitution for the Federation of Earth (1968, 1991) is very short on rights and presents an approach so moderate that its supporters seek to amalgamate with the UN. The Constitution for the Universal State of the Earth (USE), whose Constitutional Convention I chaired at the World Philosophical Forum in Athens and brought into being on 7 October 2015 (see *Peace for our Time*, 2018, pp.46–50), has a democratic deficit. It is aimed at its paid-up members, not all world citizens through the UN, and it will take decades for paid-up members to be in sufficient quantity to form a world majority, or even the 100,000 members the USE has to reach for it to be formally recognised, according to its constitution.

The World State my works and this Constitution introduce
My work within political science/international politics and statecraft draws on my early study of Roman Law and of Justinian I's 6th-century *Codex Justinianus* (Code of Justinian), the Roman Empire's codification of World Law (the law of the known world) that is the Roman World State's equivalent to this Constitution. My pioneering of Universalism has led me in the direction of this Constitution for a new World State arguably since *The Fire and the Stones* (my study of the rise and fall of civilizations) appeared in 1991 with an 'Introduction to the New Universalism'; and certainly since work I was doing in 2006, which culminated in my section on political Universalism in *The New Philosophy of Universalism* (2009). My books *The World Government* (2010) and *World State* (2018), which includes an updating of the evidence and data on which a World State should be based, are introductions to the new World State, which I have named the United Federation of the World (UF).

When it comes into existence the UF will be a partly-federal, democratically-elected world government with an inter-national World Parliamentary Assembly (an elected lower house that will initially be based in the UN General Assembly) and a supranational, federal World Commission and World Senate (an elected upper house). The hyphen in 'inter-national' suggests a secondary meaning that distinguishes it from 'supranational': 'between [Latin *inter*] nation-states', as distinct from 'above [Latin *supra*] nation-states'. As I see it, the World Parliamentary Assembly will eventually replace the UN General Assembly, and under the new federal arrangement the United Nations, UN, will be replaced by the United Federation of the World, UF.

Three reasons for naming the World State the 'United Federation of the World'

The name 'United Federation of the World' is the most appropriate name for a new World State for the following three reasons, which take possible alternative names into account:

1. *Name to reflect partial, not total, federation.* The word 'federation' comes from the Latin *'foedus'*, meaning 'league, covenant'. So a 'federation' is "the action of uniting in a league or covenant", "a union of several states under a federal government, each retaining control of its own internal affairs" (*Shorter Oxford English Dictionary*). In other words, a federation is a union of partially-self-governing states or regions under a central (federal) government. Under the United Federation of the World, all the existing nation-states will remain internally independent but will be subject to central federal control in seven areas. In Appendix A2 in *World State* I list 27 federations that involve unions of several states. These include the United States of America. As the Federation this Constitution will bring in includes all nation-states it may seem to resemble a 'United States of the World'. However, in a 'United States of the World' the federal control would be total, over everything outside the internal administration of the nation-states, whereas the federal element of the United Federation of the World is partial, limited, restricted to the seven federal goals listed in Article 1 of this Constitution (which were first stated in my books *The World Government* and *The Secret American Dream*).

2. *Name to reflect Tennyson's vision and anthem.* In the name 'United Federation of the World', 'United' echoes the 'United' in 'the United Nations'; 'Federation' suggests a union of all nation-states under a federal government limited to the seven federal goals; and 'the World' emphasises that the federation is of all the nation-states and extant civilizations in the whole world. It is the "Federation of the world" the English poet Tennyson foresaw in 'Locksley Hall' (1842), which

is in the anthem (see Article 133): 'United (as in 'United Nations') + Tennyson's "Federation of the world".

3. *Name to reflect solution to, not causes of, world's problems.* My introduction to the United Federation of the World, *World State* (in which Part One is titled 'Beyond the Nation-State'), makes clear that sovereign nation-states are the cause of the world's problems, notably the problems of wars, nuclear weapons, refugees and migrants, and that the solution to these problems requires a federal, supranational level of government that is strong enough to achieve the seven federal goals: to abolish war, impose disarmament, share energy, tackle disease, famine and poverty, and sort out global warming and financial crises. As competing nation-states have caused the world's problems and the solution to the world's problems is the seven federal goals and a limited federalism of all the world's nation-states, it is better that the new World State should be named the 'United Federation of the World' (which focuses on the solution) than the 'Federation of Nation-States' (which focuses on the problems and would be a confusing name as it suggests a total rather than a partial federation and as there have been 27 federations of nation-states). (I referred descriptively to a "Federation of nation-states" in *Peace for our Time,* 2018, p.99, quoting my paper 'Urgent Global Problems, Inactive Nation-States and Decisive Supranationalism' which can be found in Appendix 6 of that work and has been online since soon after it was written on 22–23 September 2016. However, my descriptive reference was not intended to be a name for the new World State.)

Failure of the inter-national UN to prevent wars
The United Federation of the World (or UF) will need to be much stronger than the existing inter-national United Nations, which has no supranational power and is really just a debating chamber for nation-states and a club where world leaders can meet. The UN has failed to prevent 162 wars since 1945, of which a shocking number of 72 wars are still continuing at present (for the evidence, see Appendix C6 in *World State*) and has failed to control the 2017 tally of 14,900 nuclear weapons.

On the subject of nation-states causing wars, President Trump's strong and statesman-like, internationalist address to the UN General Assembly on 18 September 2017 was about the need for secure and prosperous sovereign nation-states, national self-interest. In a place valuing peace he attacked North Korea, Venezuela, Iran, and the Islamic jihadist organisations, and threatened to destroy North Korea. There was no word on the need for a federal supranationalism that could bring lasting peace, and unsurprisingly the horrified delegates of the UN General Assembly did not persistently interrupt his speech with applause as they did when President Obama addressed them. As could be seen from their response, the world is crying out for a vision of unity that goes beyond self-interested nation-states and wars. Only a body with some supranational authority can achieve the seven goals.

Precedents legally sound
In assembling this Constitution I have consulted the precedents listed in Appendix 1, which contain wording that has been tried and tested over many years and found to be legally sound. I have amalgamated the thinking in these precedents, and where possible I have echoed the legally tried and tested phrases. This Constitution and its Articles can therefore be seen to have evolved from the precedents and their legally sound Articles. For full coverage of the thinking behind this Constitution's presentation of the United Federation of the World, see my companion volume *World State: An Introduction to the United Federation of the World*.

Need for a Constitutional Convention in the UN General Assembly
No constitution has force until it is ratified. As this Constitution for the United Federation of the World will have to be ratified, there will need to be a Constitutional Convention in the UN General Assembly to approve and no doubt amend its Articles, and at that stage a committee of lawyers will comb through this Constitution. It is my hope that the UN Secretary-General's office will look at this Constitution in conjunction with *World State*, and allow me to give a presentation to the UN General Assembly to initiate this process.

26, 30 August; 1, 28–29 September; 2, 7, 9–11 October 2017

CONSTITUTION

FOR THE

UNITED FEDERATION OF THE WORLD

PREAMBLE

We, the assembled peoples of the World – resolved to form a federal union of humankind; inaugurate a universal peace, freedom from war and menacing weapons among all nation-states; redistribute earth's natural resources and energy equitably; protect the environment from pollution and global warming; banish disease and famine; consolidate wealth, prosperity and financial security; eliminate poverty; advance universal justice and welfare, tolerance, human rights and social progress for the common good; preserve all civilizations' religious traditions; and found a new epoch of human unity – do ordain this Constitution to establish the United Federation of the World.

CHAPTER I: PURPOSES AND PRINCIPLES

Article 1 – Purposes
The Purposes of the United Federation of the World shall be:

- to create a World State with a federal, supranational level that is strong enough to abolish war and enforce universal disarmament;
- to implement the seven federal goals that will:

  1. bring peace between nation-states, and disarmament;
  2. share natural resources and energy;
  3. solve environmental problems such as global warming;
  4. end disease;
  5. end famine;
  6. solve the world's financial crisis; and
  7. redistribute wealth to eliminate poverty;

- to devise worldwide solutions to the problems of refugees and migrants, starvation and poverty, all of which are

consequences of destructive war; and
- to guarantee the fundamental and equal human rights and freedoms of all peoples and to work for the common good and welfare of all humankind.

Article 2 – Principles
The United Federation of the World, in pursuance of the Purposes stated in Article 1, and acting in accordance with the following Principles, shall:

- recognise the sovereign equality of all its Member States, each of which shall be internally independent but externally subject to the seven federal goals while remaining free in all other external relations;
- establish a bicameral legislature – with a lower house at the inter-national level between nation-states and an upper house at the supranational, federal level – that in conjunction with the executive World Commission will enact the seven federal goals among all member nation-states;
- implement universal peace, enforce disarmament and organise the dismantling of all nuclear weapons, and from the resulting savings in expenditure on wars and weapons enhance all Member States' prosperity and their implementation of the seven federal goals;
- strengthen the fundamental and equal human rights and freedoms and initiatives for universal welfare and the common good in all its Member States and enforce them through its judiciary;
- follow the vision of unity of Universalism, which relates all humankind's universal activities in all disciplines to the hidden order and underlying unity of the universe at both secular and metaphysical levels; acknowledges all religious traditions, which are followed by some 5.8 billion of the world's peoples, and the mysterious Light which is common to all and is the essence of religious Universalism; and grasps

that all peoples and individuals belong to a united humankind and are entitled to the fundamental human rights of freedom, equality, enlightenment, democracy and justice, and that the best expression of such a vision of political Universalism is a World State; and

- support all peoples' drive to self-improvement, self-betterment, self-transcendence, self-transformation and higher consciousness, through which all can attain personal inner calm, serenity and a sense that life has a meaning and purpose; and their desire to live in harmony with the universe, which universal peace and the resulting harmony of all world peoples will assist.

CHAPTER II: MEMBERSHIP

Article 3 – UN Member States
The Member States of the United Federation of the World shall be all the nation-states that are members of the United Nations at the time when the United Federation of the World is brought into existence by the ratification of this Constitution in accordance with Articles 140–145 and particularly Article 143.

Article 4 – Non-UN Member States
Membership of the United Federation of the World shall also include other nation-states formally regarded as non-UN-members, dependent territories outside the UN, disputed territories and island groups with low populations (listed in Appendix 2).

Article 5 – Suspension of a Member State
A Member State of the United Federation of the World against which preventive or enforcement action has been taken by the World

Executive Council may be suspended from exercising the rights and privileges of membership by the World Parliamentary Assembly upon the recommendation of the World Executive Council.

Article 6 – Expulsion of a Member State
A Member State of the United Federation of the World which has persistently violated the Principles set out in Article 2 may be temporarily expelled from, and subsequently readmitted to, the Federation (during which time it will suffer more drastic punitive sanctions including deprival of benefits) by the World Parliamentary Assembly upon the recommendation of the World Executive Council.

CHAPTER III: STRUCTURE

Article 7 – Rights of world citizens are worldwide and all-embracing
The rights of world citizens apply throughout the world and are more all-embracing than the rights of citizens of nation-states as world citizens assume responsibility for the whole global society in the territories of all nation-states rather than just the territory of a particular nation-state.

Article 8 – Right to live under political Universalism which expresses the fundamental interconnectedness of humankind
All shall have the right to live under political Universalism which expresses the fundamental interconnectedness and new-found unity of humankind. Seen from space the earth seems to be a unified planet and it seems apparent that humankind is descended from a single cell and is fundamentally interconnected, although DNA shows that each individual is also unique. The worldwide web allows all world citizens to communicate freely with all others and implement the fundamental interconnectedness of humankind.

Article 9 – Right to live under benevolent world rulers of integrity
All shall have the right to live under benevolent world rulers of integrity who have the power to spread freedom and democracy, abolish war, famine and disease, liberate the poor from their poverty, manage scarcity of resources and extend wealth to those who would improve the lot of humanity. Leaders of a democratic World State will always have humankind's best interests at heart and seek to bring paradise to the earth, and Universalism shall be the philosophy of a good globalist World State that has Utopian ambitions for all humankind. Certain rights are inalienable – universal freedom, democracy and relief from poverty, war, famine and disease – and there is no place for self-interested world rulers or oligarchs who would appropriate the earth's resources for their own enrichment.

Article 10 – Right to live under a democratic world government
All shall have the human right to live under the United Federation of the World: a democratic world government – a World State and a supranational World Authority with legal power to declare war illegal – that shall abolish war, famine, disease and poverty. Under its political Universalism the conflicts and divisions between peoples shall be minimised and all shall be able to see beyond borders and national identities to the global identity of world citizens and the outlook under a universal World State. (See also Article 105.)

Article 11 – Seven federal goals
In accordance with Article 1, the United Federation of the World shall pursue seven federal goals and:

1. bring peace between nation-states, and disarmament;
2. share natural resources and energy so that all humankind can have a raised standard of living;
3. solve environmental problems such as global warming, which seem to be beyond self-interested nation-states;
4. end disease;

5. end famine;
6. solve the world's financial crisis; and
7. redistribute wealth to eliminate poverty.

Article 12 – Institutions at inter-national and supranational levels
The principal institutions of the United Federation of the World at the inter-national level shall be:

- The World Parliamentary Assembly (which shall replace the UN General Assembly);
- The World Executive Council (which shall replace the UN Security Council); and
- The World Council of Justice (which shall replace the International Court of Justice).

The principal institutions of the United Federation of the World at the supranational (federal) level shall be:

- The World Commission;
- The World Senate;
- The World Senatorial Committees;
- The World Openness Committee;
- The World Council of Ministers;
- The President and Presidency of the World Council of Ministers;
- The World Guidance Council;
- The World Leaders' Meetings;
- The World Bank and the World Investment Bank;
- The executive of International Lawyers;
- The World Court of Justice;
- The World Court of First Instance;
- The World Judicial Tribunals;
- The World Constitutional Court;
- The World Ombudsman; and
- The World Armed Force (or the World Rapid Reaction Force).

Most of the institutions of the United Federation of the World are on the diagram/flow chart in Appendix 5.

Article 13 – Subsidiary institutions
Subsidiary institutions may be established if deemed necessary in accordance with the Purposes and Principles of this Constitution.

Article 14 – Equality of men and women
The United Federation of the World shall place no restrictions on the eligibility of men and women to participate in any capacity and under conditions of equality in its principal and subsidiary institutions.

Article 15 – Tripartite separation of powers: legislative, executive and judicial institutions
The United Federation of the World shall partly exist and operate at the inter-national level (between nation-states) and shall partly exist and operate at the supranational (federal) level. At both levels it shall operate a tripartite separation of powers through legislative, executive and judicial institutions.

Article 16 – Representation of humankind through institutions
The United Federation of the World shall represent all humankind in all nation-states and civilizations at the inter-national level through its elected representatives in:

- its legislative World Parliamentary Assembly;
- its executive World Executive Council; and
- its judicial World Court of Justice (a replacement for the International Court of Justice).

It shall further represent all humankind in all nation-states and civilizations at the supranational (federal) level through its elected representatives in:

- its legislative World Commission and World Senate;
- its executive World Council of Ministers and Presidency; and
- its judicial World Court of Justice and World Court of First Instance.

CHAPTER IV: THE INTER-NATIONAL LEVEL

Article 17 – Tripartite institutions at inter-national level
The United Federation of the World's inter-national structure shall operate a tripartite separation of powers through its main institutions: the legislative World Parliamentary Assembly; the executive World Executive Council; and the judicial World Court of Justice.

Article 18 – Tripartite functions at inter-national level
Within its legislative and executive institutions there shall be a further tripartite separation of functions:

- the World Parliamentary Assembly shall make recommendations (as does the UN General Assembly);
- the World Executive Council shall decide (as does the UN Security Council); and
- the UN Secretary-General and his Secretariat (the inter-national equivalent to the World Commission during the transitional period) shall implement.

1. Legislature

Article 19 – World Parliamentary Assembly and operational powers
The UN General Assembly shall be converted into an elected World Parliamentary Assembly of the United Federation of the World at the inter-national level (between nation-states). The World Parliamentary Assembly shall be a lower house at the inter-national level. It shall legislate supranationally in conjunction with the World Senate and act as a global legislature in some sessions as well as representing individual Member States' parliaments.

Article 20 – Allocation of seats in World Parliamentary Assembly
The allocation of the World Parliamentary Assembly's seats shall be decided by taking account of and adjusting for national and territorial arrangements, countries' populations, nuclear influence and Permanent Membership of the UN Security Council. The presumption is that there shall eventually be 850 seats, with provision for more if future developments require. The allocation of seats shall be in accordance with the allocation of seats listed in Appendix 2.

Article 21 – Offshoots of UN General Assembly
All the offshoots of the UN General Assembly shall continue to operate during the transitional period. These are the Economic and Social Council, the International Criminal Court, the International Court of Justice and the UN institutions (UNDP, UNHCR, UNICEF and UNEP) and specialised agencies (FAO, UNESCO, WHO and WTO).

Article 22 – World political parties
In keeping with a democratically-elected system all representatives of the World Parliamentary Assembly shall belong to one of the World Political Parties. These shall hold different views on all the world's issues, including the management of world resources and energy

supply, and the level of world taxation and redistribution. There shall be a World Centre/Right Party; a World Socialist Centre/Left Party; a World Liberal Centre/Left Party; a World Green Party; a World Far-Left Party; a World Far-Right Party; and a Worldsceptic Party (a Party for World Sceptics). From the outset all nation-states shall participate in federal world elections, regardless of whether they are internal democracies or dictatorships.

2. Executive

Article 23 – World Executive Council
The UN Security Council shall be converted into a veto-less World Executive Council of the United Federation of the World. It shall continue to have 5 Permanent Members (the People's Republic of China, the French Republic, Russian Federation, the United Kingdom of Great Britain and Northern Ireland, and the United States of America, the same as the 5 Permanent Members of the UN Security Council) and 12 Non-Permanent Members elected for two-year terms.

Article 24 – Allocation of seats on World Executive Council
The 17 representatives of the World Executive Council (the replacement for the UN Security Council) shall be elected by the World Parliamentary Assembly. Five representatives shall represent each of the Permanent Members, 5 of the next 10 largest nation-states (see Appendix 1, A and C) shall have rotational representation (so that all 10 are represented, but only 5 at any one time), and the other 7 shall be chosen by the World Parliamentary Assembly from representatives of other nation-states (see Appendix 1, C and D). The veto-less World Executive Council shall decide whether each stage of the disarmament process has been satisfactorily completed.

Article 25 – Tripartite operational powers at inter-national and supranational levels
The tripartite inter-national structure shall continue to field all conflicts requiring resolution in the first instance. Only the intractable problems on which the World Executive Council cannot reach agreement shall be passed up to the supranational level. The UN Peacekeeping Force shall continue to operate under the World Executive Council (as under the UN Security Council) in containable conflicts that do not require the involvement of the supranational level.

3. Judiciary

Article 26 – World Court of Justice
The International Court of Justice shall be converted into a United Federation of the World's World Court of Justice. This court shall exist at both inter-national and supranational levels (see Article 40). At the inter-national level, the World Court of Justice, based in the Peace Palace, The Hague, Netherlands (the UN's primary judicial institution), shall continue to settle legal disputes submitted to it by Member States and give advisory opinions on legal questions placed before it by the World Parliamentary Assembly (the replacement for the UN General Assembly). The World Court of Justice shall continue to resolve legal problems arising from conflicts in the first instance (like the tripartite inter-national World Parliamentary Assembly, the World Executive Council and the Secretary-General).

CHAPTER V: THE SUPRANATIONAL LEVEL

Article 27 – Tripartite institutions at supranational level
The supranational level shall preside over all Member States: all nation-states and their civilizations. The supranational structure shall operate

a tripartite separation of powers through its main institutions: the legislative World Commission, which shall make recommendations connected with the seven federal goals, and World Senate, which shall turn recommendations connected with the seven federal goals into laws; the executive World Council of Ministers, which shall make decisions on recommendations connected with the seven federal goals; and the judicial World Court of Justice and World Court of First Instance.

1. Legislature

Article 28 – World Commission and operational powers
The World Commission shall be the supranational World Authority that conducts the United Federation of the World. It shall propose laws, monitor the implementation of all directives and world policies, and represent the World Authority in the inter-national institutions of global governance (the G8, the OECD, the Bank for International Settlements, the World Bank, the International Monetary Fund, the World Trade Organization and all the agencies of the UN). The World Commission's proposals shall all relate to the implementation and achievement of the seven federal goals, which include the enforcement of peace and disarmament and guarantee the security of all nation-states.

Article 29 – Allocation of seats in World Commission
The World Commission shall be drawn from all regions of the world. It shall be composed of 27 members, the maximum number that can sit comfortably round a table and take part in World-Authority meetings to enforce peace and conduct a world government. The 27 seats on the World Commission shall be allocated after taking account of regional representation, population percentages, topographical extent, Permanent Membership of the UN Security Council, and possession of nuclear warheads to be disarmed; in accordance with the allocation listed in Appendix 3.

Article 30 – World Senate and operational powers
The World Senate shall be a directly-elected upper house. The World Senate shall work with the World Parliamentary Assembly in the same way that the upper and lower houses work together in the US Congress. The relationship between the World Senate and the World Commission shall be like that of the European Parliament and the European Commission – only there shall be a bicameral system, one chamber (the World Parliamentary Assembly) being at inter-national level and the higher chamber (the World Senate) being at supranational level and dedicated to implementing the seven goals of the supranational authority and to passing the laws needed to establish and enforce universal peace. The senators shall work closely with the World Commission, and with the World Parliamentary Assembly. The Assembly shall send up to the World Commission matters beyond its competence, including conflicts which require enforcement, and the World Commission shall pass its proposals connected with the seven federal goals to the World Senate for them to become law. The World Senate shall turn the World Commission's proposals into laws and thereby implement the seven federal goals. Some senators shall be experts in international law.

Article 31 – Allocation of seats in World Senate
The World Senate shall be elected on a basis of regional zones. There shall be 46 zonal constituencies, each of which shall elect 2 senators, making a total of 92 senators. The regional zones shall include the nation-states in each region, and the allocation of constituencies shall take account of regional representation, population percentages, topographical area, possession of nuclear weapons to be disarmed, political clout and environmental considerations; in accordance with the allocation listed in Appendix 4.

Article 32 – World Senatorial Committees
There shall be World Senatorial Committees to monitor the implementation of the seven federal goals:

15

1. *Goal 1*

    There shall be World Senatorial Committees to implement goal 1: a World Committee of the Regions, a World Economic and Social Committee, a World Peace Enforcement Committee and a World Disarmament Enforcement Committee.

2. *Goals 2–7*

    There shall also be World Senatorial Committees to implement goals 2–7: a World Resources Committee, a World Energy Committee, a World Environmental Committee, a World Disease Committee, a World Famine Committee, a World Finance Committee, a World Poverty Committee and a World Population Committee.

These World Senatorial Committees shall liaise with the World Commission, the World Court of Justice and the World Parliamentary Assembly.

Article 33 – World Openness Committee and operational powers

The World Openness Committee is a very important World Senatorial Committee. It shall control the agencies of the *élites*. The World Openness Committee shall scrutinize all candidates seeking to be world officials in terms of their possible links to the *élites'* self-interested world agendas and their known wish to control the world's natural resources and energy supply.

1. *Élite-owned energy*

    Working in conjunction with the World Resources Committee, this World Openness Committee shall seek to return all *élite*-owned energy to the peoples of the World.

2. *Élitist agencies*

    The World Openness Committee shall receive advance copies of all agendas of élitist agencies such as the Bilderberg Group and Trilateral Commission, and all minutes of their meetings.

Two members of the World Openness Committee shall attend all meetings of these agencies and report back to the World Commission to ensure that the work of all agencies is transparent. The *élites* shall not be involved in decision-making.

Article 34 – Executive of International Lawyers
The executive of International Lawyers shall help the World Commission, the World Senate and the World Parliamentary Assembly turn the World Commission's proposals into international laws. It shall liaise with the World Peace Enforcement Committee and the World Court of Justice.

2. Executive

Article 35 – World Council of Ministers and operational powers
The World Council of Ministers shall act as the collective executive power of the Member States. It shall meet as the World Cabinet under the leadership of the World President. It shall be responsible for making decisions on recommendations connected with the seven federal goals before passing the recommendations back to the World Commission to be passed on to the World Senate to be turned into laws:

1. *29 World Ministers*
    The World Council of Ministers shall consist of 29 World Ministers, the maximum number that can sit comfortably round a Cabinet table. The World Ministers shall be drawn from the representatives of the World Parliamentary Assembly who belong to the World Political Party that has won the four-yearly world elections.

2. *29 World Departments*
    The World Ministers shall represent 29 World Departments,

each of which shall work closely with the World Senatorial Committees that operate in its field. The World Departments shall be:

- World Finance;
- World Treasury;
- World Peace;
- World Disarmament;
- World Resources;
- World Environment;
- World Climate Change;
- World Health (ending disease);
- World Food (ending famine, implementing crop-growing programs);
- World Regions, Communities and Families;
- World Work and Pensions;
- World Housing;
- World Economic Development;
- World Regional Aid and International Development (ending financial crises);
- World Poverty (eliminating poverty);
- World Population Containment (not reduction);
- World Energy Regulation;
- World Transport (world aviation, roads and rail);
- World Law;
- World Oceans;
- World Space;
- World Education;
- World Citizenship (law and order);
- World Culture and History;
- World Sport;
- World Unity in Diversity;
- World Dependent Territories;
- World Foreign Policies (liaising with Member States' Foreign Ministers); and
- World Human Rights and Freedom (guaranteeing

individual freedoms, including freedom from population reduction under the new system).

Article 36 – World President and Presidency of World Council of Ministers, nomination and election
The World President shall be elected every four years (like the President of the United States). The Presidential election shall be contested by every World Political Party, and all voters in all world constituencies shall vote. Presidential candidates shall be nominated by the World Political Parties, and each shall be vetted by the World Commission and the senatorial World Openness Committee for suitability, integrity and lack of links to the élitist agencies. The world election campaign shall involve visits to the main regions, and there shall be a world ballot. The successful directly-elected World President shall be sworn in by the World Commission and a judge of the World Court of Justice:

1. *Unelected rotational appointment of World President undemocratic*
   There is a view, held among undemocratic, one-party nation-states, that the World President should be appointed by the World Council of Ministers by qualified majority voting for a term of two and a half years, and that the President can be removed by the same voting procedure. On this view, the Presidency of the World Council of Ministers should rotate automatically among the Member States and over a period of time should represent every continent. On this view, the first rotation should start with the 5 Permanent Members of the World Executive Council, and the role of the President should in no sense be equivalent to the office of head of state. Rather, the role should merely be to be a *primus inter pares* (first among equals) among other heads of government of the Member States. However, this view is insufficiently democratic to be acceptable to the democratically-elected United Federation of the World and remains an option hankered after by dictatorial nation-states opposed to democratic accountability.

2. *World President and operational powers*
The President shall be primarily responsible for: co-ordinating the work of the World Council of Ministers and chairing its meetings; presenting the annual budget, the legislative proposals and annual report of the World Council of Ministers to the World Parliamentary Assembly and the World Senate; representing the World Council of Ministers at the World Leaders' Meetings; and leading the World Cabinet and the World Council of Ministers' decision-making on recommendations connected with the seven federal goals. (See Article 35.)

Article 37 – World Guidance Council and operational powers
There shall be a World Guidance Council of elder statesmen and distinguished world figures. They shall meet every three months, or more frequently if a crisis demands, to advise the World Commission, World Senate, and World Council of Ministers. These wise elders shall be chosen on merit and expertise, with consideration being paid to regional representation, population percentages and political clout, on the recommendation of the World Commission, World Senate and World Council of Ministers.

Article 38 – World Leaders' Meetings for heads of governments and 13 main regions
There shall be World Leaders' Meetings for the heads of government of all the Member States and, sometimes, their foreign ministers. There shall be a particular Regional Leaders' Meeting for the leaders of the 13 main regions, which are based on the 14 living civilizations (13 because South America includes two living civilizations, the separate Andean and Meso-American civilizations): North America; Europe; Japan; Oceania; China; Tibet; the Russian Federation; South America; Islam (representing Muslims in West, Central, South and South-East Asia and North and North-East Africa, and focusing on Indonesia and India which have the world's largest Muslim populations); Africa;

India; South-East Asia; and Central Asia. A member of the World Commission shall be present at all meetings of World Leaders, along with the Minister of a Department and a senator.

Article 39 – World Bank and World Investment Bank and operational powers
The World Bank and World Investment Bank shall be overhauled to operate at a supranational level. The World Bank shall continue to make loans to poorer countries for capital programs to reduce poverty. The World Commission shall draw on these world banking institutions to fund and achieve its seven goals:

1. to bring peace and complete disarmament;
2. begin a phased redistribution of humankind's resources and energy supply to even the disparities between regions;
3. ease environmental problems such as global warming and manage common resources including outer space and oceans;
4. end disease;
5. end famine;
6. solve the world's financial crisis; and
7. redistribute wealth to help poverty.

The World Commission shall guarantee a minimum standard of living for all humankind on a phased basis, and a World Development Authority shall grant interest-free loans to assist the economic and social development of under-developed areas.

3. Judiciary

Article 40 – World Court of Justice, composition and operational powers
The World Court of Justice shall have 25 judges. These shall be chosen on the same basis as the World Commission but excluding the seconded experts from the World Bank and agencies of global government:

1. *Actions brought by World Commission*
   The World Court of Justice's primary function shall be to hear actions brought by the World Commission against a Member State for breaking a directive. One of its briefs shall be to rule against self-interested *élites'* use of the world's resources and energy supply. It shall also rule on conflicts and fulfil a role of conflict resolution by ordering a Member State to desist from actions that could result in war. It shall hear cases regarding conflicts between Member States referred up to the World Parliamentary Assembly and brought by the World Commission before the Court.

2. *Legal disputes*
   The World Court of Justice shall rule on legal disputes between Member States and between the World Commission and institutions and agencies. It shall further disarmament. It shall hear complaints against actions taken by a world institution. It shall interpret world law at the request of national courts, and respond to direct petitions.

Article 41 – World Court of First Instance and operational powers
The World Court of First Instance shall exist alongside the World Court of Justice to ease the World Court of Justice's workload. The World Court of First Instance shall hear actions brought by citizens and companies against the World Commission for its deeds or failure to act, and shall hear actions for damages against the World Commission.

Article 42 – World Judicial Tribunals and operational powers
There shall be a substructure of World Judicial Tribunals under the World Court of Justice, which shall further take pressure off the World Court of Justice. These World Judicial Tribunals shall hear cases in which world laws needed to be enforced, and shall enforce international laws.

Article 43 – World Constitutional Court and operational powers
The World Constitutional Court shall be the supreme authority regarding the interpretation of this Constitution, and the defending and protecting of the fundamental rights and freedoms of all world citizens.

Article 44 – World Ombudsman and operational powers
With the exception of the World Court of Justice and the World Judicial Tribunals of the United Federation of the World, all world citizens or world organisations shall have the right to refer to the World Ombudsman cases of maladministration in the activities of the institutions, bodies, offices or agencies of the Federation. (See also Article 114.)

Article 45 – World Armed Force (or World Rapid Reaction Force) and operational powers
The World Armed Force (or World Rapid Reaction Force) of 200,000–400,000 troops shall serve the World Commission, the World Council of Ministers, the World Senate, the World Parliamentary Assembly, the World Executive Council, the World Court of Justice and the World Constitutional Court. The World Armed Force shall be used to enforce laws for the World Commission just as the UN's Peacekeeping Force has been used to enforce laws for the Security Council. There shall be a reserve force of 300,000–600,000 troops.

CHAPTER VI: PEACE DIVIDEND

Article 46 – Initial funding from the UN and Member States
The funding of the United Federation of the World shall initially be partly afforded out of the existing budget of the UN. Funding of the UN General Assembly shall be switched to the World Parliamentary

Assembly. There shall be one budget for the entire United Federation of the World and all its committees, agencies and operations, and this will be considered and approved by the World Parliamentary Assembly and the World Senate. The funding of the Federation shall also be borne by the Member States as apportioned by the World Commission, the World Senate and the World Parliamentary Assembly.

Article 47 – Eventual funding from savings through reductions in military expenditure
Because the World Commission's principal goal is to abolish war and the need for expenditure on arms, all the Member States shall cut their defence budgets and divert funds from saved military expenditure amounting to trillions of dollars into funding for the supranational level. While the initial funding of the establishing of the United Federation of the World shall be covered partly by diverted UN funds and partly by money from the taxation revenues of the Member States, eventually this money shall be recouped from, replaced by and more than covered by the peace dividend: savings through reductions in military expenditure.

Article 48 – Surrender of enough sovereignty to achieve the seven federal goals
By nominating members of the World Commission and electing senators to the World Senate and representatives to the World Parliamentary Assembly, the Member States will be accepting the authority of the World Commission and the new supranational structure. All Member States shall surrender some sovereignty along with their right to fight wars and stockpile nuclear warheads, but it will only be a relatively small amount: just enough sovereignty to secure the achievement of the seven supranational goals and the peace dividend.

Article 49 – Life under a world government achieving the seven federal goals
The supranational, federal level shall be above the inter-national level

in which associations of nation-states (such as the United Nations and NATO) have tried to keep the peace between nation-states. From the perspective of nation-states, the Member States, life will be little different from how it was before the United Federation of the World. However, the seven goals will have been implemented. There will not be a world government with total sovereignty and control over all lives, but a world government that will operate at a supranational level and permit the inter-national level to continue as before except in the seven areas relating to the seven goals and the peace dividend. The supranational level shall only be federal in the areas of the seven goals.

Article 50 – No adverse impact on individual liberty
After the establishment of the United Federation of the World there will be more democracy and an end to the élitist abuses of global governance. There will be no adverse impact on individual liberty outside the achievement of the seven goals. Under the United Federation of the World and its peace dividend humankind will come to have an awareness of its unity, and its structure of political Universalism will unite humankind.

Article 51 – All civilizations will flow into one worldwide civilization but will continue their rising-and-falling pattern at the inter-national level
After the establishment of the United Federation of the World all civilizations will flow into one worldwide civilization at the supranational level (see the chart in Appendix 6) in the sense that they will all be under the technical rule of the World Commission, the World Senate, the World Parliamentary Assembly, the World Executive Council, the World President and the World Council of Ministers. Yet the supranational structure under the peace dividend will be sufficiently remote to allow civilizations to continue as before at the lower inter-national level. Civilizations will continue their rising-and-falling pattern at the inter-national level.

CHAPTER VII: RIGHTS AND FREEDOMS

Article 52 – Entitlement to all rights and freedoms guaranteed by the United Federation of the World
Under the United Federation of the World all humankind shall be seen to be the unity that it is, and all shall be entitled to all the rights and freedoms guaranteed by the United Federation of the World and enjoyed under the rule of worldwide law. World citizens' rights and freedoms are universal, fundamental and indivisible, and the categorisation of rights invariably invokes freedoms, and *vice versa*.

Article 53 – Right to life
All shall have the right to life.

Article 54 – Prohibition of death penalty
No one shall be subjected to the death penalty, or executed.

Article 55 – Prohibition of torture
No one shall be subjected to torture or to cruel, inhuman or degrading treatment or punishment.

Article 56 – Prohibition of arbitrary arrest and detention
No one shall be subjected to arbitrary arrest, detention, imprisonment or exile. All shall have the right to freedom from groundless stop-and-search.

Article 57 – Right to freedom from war
All shall have the right to freedom from war and to world peace.

Article 58 – Right to freedom from genocide
All shall have the right to freedom from genocide and violent (as opposed to planned) population control or reduction.

Article 59 – Right to freedom from poverty, famine and disease
All shall have the right to freedom from poverty, famine and disease.

Article 60 – Prohibition of murder and rape
All shall have the right to freedom from murder and rape. All human beings have the right to live in freedom from all kinds of violence in both public and private life.

Article 61 – Prohibition of slavery and forced labour
No one shall be held in slavery or servitude, or be compelled to perform forced or compulsory labour. Slavery and the slave trade, and trafficking in human beings, shall be prohibited in all their forms.

Article 62 – Right to integrity of person
All shall have respect for their physical and mental integrity and shall not be subjected to medical and biological procedures involving their person without their free and informed consent. Female genital mutilation shall be prohibited. (See also Article 96.)

Article 63 – Right to self-defence
All shall have the right to self-defence.

Article 64 – Right not to be removed, expelled or extradited
No one shall be removed, expelled or extradited to a Member State where there is a serious risk of being subjected to the death penalty,

torture or other inhuman or degrading treatment or punishment. Collective expulsions are prohibited.

Article 65 – Right to asylum
All shall have the right to seek and to enjoy asylum from persecution in other Member States.

Article 66 – Right to freedom of movement and residence
All world citizens of the United Federation of the World shall have the right to move and reside freely – the right to freedom of movement and residence – within the borders and territory of each Member State, subject to the ability of each Member State's internal circumstances and infrastructures to accommodate and cope with new migrants. All shall have the right to leave any Member State, including their own, and to return to their Member State. The United Federation of the World guarantees freedom of movement, residence and work in all Member States (see also Article 78.2) without requiring passports, visas or travel documents, and to have diplomatic and consular protection, subject to each Member State's ability to accommodate new migrants.

Article 67 – Right to dual nationality
During the transitional period while the United Federation of the World is being established world citizens shall have the right to dual nationality: to citizenship of both the United Federation of the World and of their own Member State. Citizenship of a Member State shall co-exist with the Federation's world citizenship. Eventually, citizenship of Member States shall fall away. Until then all shall have the right to dual nationality and no one shall be arbitrarily deprived of, or denied the right to change, any nationality.

Article 68 – Right to liberty and security
All shall have the right to liberty and security of person.

Article 69 – Right to marry and found a family

All shall have the right and freedom to marry and found a family.

Article 70 – Right to private and family life

All shall have the right to a private and family life, home and communications, and to have these treated with respect. All shall be protected by the law from arbitrary interference with their privacy, family, home or correspondence, and from attacks upon their honour and reputation. All families shall be provided with legal, economic and social protection.

Article 71 – Prohibition of child labour and protection of young people at work

The employment of children is prohibited. The minimum age of admission to employment shall not be lower than the minimum school-leaving age. Young people admitted to work shall have working conditions appropriate to their age and be protected from economic exploitation and any work likely to harm their safety, health, mental, moral or social development or to interfere with their education.

Article 72 – Freedom of thought, conscience and religion

All shall have the right to freedom of thought, conscience and religion. This right includes freedom to change their religion or belief, and freedom, either alone or in community with others and in public or private, to manifest one's religion or belief in teaching, practice, worship and observance.

Article 73 – Freedom of expression and information

All shall have the right to freedom of expression. This right shall include freedom to hold opinions and to receive and impart information and ideas without interference by public authorities and regardless of frontiers. All shall have the right to participate in the information society and to access the internet or any other future means of communication without interference by public authorities or private groups.

Article 74 – Protection of personal data
All shall have the right to the protection of personal and confidential data. All shall have the right of access to data collected about them, and the right to have it rectified.

Article 75 – Freedom of assembly
All shall have the right to freedom of peaceful assembly and association, including political, trade union and civic assembly and association.

Article 76 – Freedom of the arts and sciences
All shall have the right of access to art and science:

1. *Right to freedom from constraint*
   The arts and scientific research shall be free from constraint. Academic freedom shall be respected.

2. *Right to participate*
   All shall have the right to participate freely in the cultural life of the community, to enjoy the arts and to share in scientific advancement and its benefits.

3. *Right to recognition and support*
   Artists and scientists shall have a right to recognition and support. As art deepens human experience of the beauty and harmony of the universe and science enables humankind to master the power of nature, the United Federation of the World shall recognise that artists, poets, writers, philosophers and scientists enable humankind to progress and shall ensure financial support at Federal, national, municipal and community levels for their creative activities and scientific research.

Article 77 – Right to education
All shall have the right to education:

1. *Right to all aspects of education*
   This right shall include entitlement to free compulsory education and vocational and continuing training, and access to technical and professional education and to the possibility of higher education, subject to merit.

2. *Right to development of personality and awareness of human rights*
   Education shall develop the students' personalities and strengthen their awareness of, and respect for, human rights and fundamental freedoms, and for the spirit of peace and world unity.

3. *Right to choose kind of education*
   All shall have the right to choose the kind of education that shall be given to their children, and to ensure that the education and teaching of their children conforms to their religious, philosophical and pedagogical convictions, in accordance with the national laws governing such rights and freedoms. All shall have the right to found educational establishments with due respect for democratic principles.

Article 78 – Right to work and freedom to choose an occupation
All shall have the right to work and to pursue a freely chosen occupation:

1. *Right to seek employment*
   All shall have the right to seek employment, to have the right of access to a free placement service, to free choice of employment and to protection against unemployment.

2. *Right to work in any Member State*
   All shall have the right to work and provide services in any Member State of the United Federation of the World, subject

to its ability to accommodate new migrants. (See also Article 66.)

3. *Right to equal pay for equal work*
   All shall have the right to equal pay for equal work without discrimination. (See also Article 91.)

4. *Right to just and favourable remuneration*
   All shall have the right to just and favourable remuneration. This can be supplemented by social protection.

5. *Right to form and join trade unions*
   All shall have the right to form and to join trade unions for the protection of their interests.

6. *Right to protection from unjustified dismissal*
   All shall have the right to protection from unjustified dismissal, and the right to paid maternity leave and to parental leave following the birth or adoption of a child.

Article 79 – Freedom to establish and conduct a business
All shall have the freedom to establish and conduct a business in accordance with Federation law and national laws and practices.

Article 80 – Fair and just working conditions
All shall have the right to working conditions which respect health and safety and dignity; to the limitation of their maximum working hours; to daily and weekly rest periods; and to an annual period of paid leave. All shall have the right to rest and leisure, including reasonable limitation of working hours and periodic holidays with pay.

Article 81 – Right of collective bargaining and action
All workers and employees and their respective organisations shall

have, in accordance with Federation law and national laws and practices, the right to negotiate and conclude collective agreements at the appropriate levels and, in cases of conflict of interest, to take collective action to defend their interests, including strike action.

Article 82 – Right to property
All shall have the right to own, use, dispose of and bequeath property alone or in association with others. None shall be arbitrarily deprived of their property. All forms of property, including intellectual property, shall be protected.

Article 83 – Right to social welfare and social security
All shall have the right to social welfare and social security:

1. *Right to adequate standard of living, welfare and social security*
   All shall have the right to a standard of living that is adequate for personal and family health and well-being, including food, clothing, housing, medical care and protective healthcare, care for all children and necessary social services. All shall have the right to social security in the event of unemployment, sickness, disability, widowhood, old age or lack of livelihood in circumstances beyond control.

2. *Right to a phased-in universal basic income*
   All shall have the right to a universal basic income in return for a contribution to world society. The United Federation of the World will achieve this goal by a phased program of subsidising full employment within the Member States.

Article 84 – Right to protection of the environment
All shall have the right to protection of the environment and the earth's ecological system in accordance with the principle of sustainable development: development of the environment that meets present

generations' needs without compromising the ability of future generations to meet their needs, so humankind can have a sustainable future in line with the principles of the United Nations' *Rio Declaration on Environment and Development.*

Article 85 – Right to visit world heritage sites
Under the United Federation of the World all shall have the right to visit historical monuments and archaeological ruins on world heritage sites and the past civilizations that produced them. Heritage sites shall be protected from damage, destruction and demolition. Protection of the environment shall extend to a cultural landscape that can inspire a universal high civilization.

Article 86 – Right to plant and grow
All shall be encouraged to protect the environment by training in gardening and the planting of trees and flowers, and supporting localised ecologically-based agriculture and the growth of crops. All shall be encouraged to remake the world as a garden, a harmonious Eden of beauty for all humans, animals, and *flora* and *fauna.*

CHAPTER VIII: EQUAL RIGHTS AND JUSTICE

Article 87 – Right of equality before the law
Under the democratic United Federation of the World's Universalism all humankind shall be seen as equal under the law and shall be entitled to the right of equality before the law and equal protection under the law. The equality of humankind is apparent to both the reason and the intuition (which perceive the unity of the universe), and to the 5.8 billion world citizens who hold a religion and have a spiritual view. All human beings are born free and are equal in spirit, dignity and rights.

Article 88 – Right to be protected against discrimination
All shall have the right to be protected against discrimination based on nationality, sex, race, colour, ethnic or social origin, genetic features, language, religion or belief, political or any other opinion, membership of a national minority, property, birth, disability, age or sexual orientation.

Article 89 – Right to humanitarian assistance
All shall have a right to humanitarian assistance.

Article 90 – Right to have diversity respected
Under the United Federation of the World all shall have the right to have their cultural, religious and linguistic diversity respected.

Article 91 – Equal rights between women and men
Equal rights between women and men shall be guaranteed in employment, work and pay in the political, economic, social, cultural and civil fields. (See also Article 78.3.)

Article 92 – Rights of children
Children shall have the right to such protection and care as is necessary for their well-being. They shall express their views freely. The United Federation of the World's legislative policy shall respect the freedoms and best interests of all children. All children shall have the right to maintain a personal relationship and direct contact with both parents on a regular basis unless special circumstances (such as violence and abuse) make that contrary to their interests.

Article 93 – Rights of the elderly
The elderly shall have the rights to lead a life of dignity and independence and to participate in social and cultural life.

Article 94 – Rights of the disabled
The disabled shall have the right to benefit from measures designed to ensure their independence, social and occupational integration and participation in the life of the community. Justice ensures that human rights and freedoms apply to all equally and fairly, and the United Federation of the World shall guarantee that there is no discrimination against the disabled in any field.

Article 95 – Right to justice and equity
All shall have the right to justice and equity along with freedom and democracy under the rule of law, which this Constitution guarantees.

Article 96 – Right to recognition as a person
All shall have the right to be recognised everywhere as a person before the law. (See also Article 62.)

Article 97 – Right to effective remedy and fair trial
All whose rights and freedoms are guaranteed by this Constitution and by the law of the United Federation of the World shall, if they are violated, have the right to an effective remedy by the United Federation of the World's, or their Member-State's, tribunals.

Article 98 – Right to be presumed innocent and to defence
All charged shall have the right to be presumed innocent until proved guilty according to law, and shall have the right of defence.

Article 99 – Rights relating to criminal offences and penalties
All shall have the right not to be held guilty of any criminal offence on account of any act or omission which did not constitute a criminal offence under national or international law at the time

when it was committed. Nor shall a heavier penalty be imposed than the one that was applicable at the time the criminal offence was committed. If, subsequent to the commission of a criminal offence the law provides for a lighter penalty, that penalty shall be applicable. The severity of penalties must not be disproportionate to the criminal offence.

Article 100 – Right not be tried or punished twice for the same criminal offence
All shall have the right not to be liable to be tried or punished again in criminal proceedings for an offence for which they have already been acquitted or convicted within the United Federation of the World in accordance with the law.

Article 101 – World Constitutional Court
All shall have the right to seek redress from the World Constitutional Court, which shall interpret, protect and defend the human rights and freedoms of all world citizens that are set out in this Constitution:

1. *Right to fair and public hearing*
   All shall be entitled to a fair and public hearing within a reasonable time by an independent and impartial tribunal previously established by law. All shall have the possibility of being advised, defended and represented.

2. *Right to legal aid*
   All shall have a right to legal aid, which shall be made available to all who lack sufficient resources in so far as such aid is necessary to ensure effective access to justice.

CHAPTER IX: WORLD CITIZENS' RIGHTS

Article 102 – Right to fair taxation
All shall have the right to a fair taxation system that promotes common welfare rather than the sale of arms that create wars, poverty and famine. An independent regulative system shall supervise fair and proper management and use of taxation at both federal and national levels to secure global social justice.

Article 103 – Right to fair banking
All shall have the right to a trustworthy, fair and transparent banking system.

Article 104 – Right to eliminate debts
The United Federation of the World shall draw up a phased plan for eliminating the Member States' long-term foreign debts, which may take decades to pay off.

Article 105 – Right to democracy
All shall have the right to democracy. The principle of democracy resides in the sovereignty of all world peoples, and civil rights, the rights of world citizens to political and social freedom and equality, shall guarantee human rights and freedoms. (See also Article 10.)

Article 106 – Right to take part in government
All shall have the right to take part in the government of the United Federation of the World and in the government of their Member State, directly or through elected representatives.

Article 107 – Right of equal access to public services
All shall have the right of equal access to public services in the United Federation of the World and their Member State.

Article 108 – Right to take part in elections
All shall have a right to take part in periodic elections which express the will of the people (the basis of the world government's authority) and shall be held on the basis of universal and equal suffrage and secret vote at federal, national and municipal levels:

1. *Right to vote and to stand as a candidate in elections*
   All shall have the right to vote and to stand as a candidate at elections to the World Parliamentary Assembly and World Senate in the Member State in which they reside, under the same conditions as nationals of that Member State.

2. *Right of representatives and senators to be elected in a free and secret ballot*
   All representatives of the World Parliamentary Assembly and senators of the World Senate shall have the right to be elected by direct universal suffrage in a free and secret ballot.

Article 109 – Right to direct democracy on legislation
All world citizens shall have a right to vote directly on legislation by means of:

- initiatives in which they shall gather signatures to advance legislation on specific statutory measures or constitutional amendments and place them on a ballot for a popular vote;
- referenda which shall allow them to place legislation that has recently been passed by a legislature on a ballot for a popular vote; and
- recall which gives them the power to remove elected officials from office before the end of their term.

Legislation by direct democracy's initiatives, referenda and recall shall co-exist alongside legislation by representational democracy in an elected legislative body which develops and passes laws.

Article 110 – Right to good administration
All shall have the right to good administration, to have their affairs handled impartially, fairly and within a reasonable time by the institutions, bodies, offices and agencies of the United Federation of the World. This right shall include:

- the right of all to be heard before any individual measure is taken that will affect them adversely;
- the right of all to have access to their file while respecting the legitimate interests of confidentiality and of professional and business secrecy; and
- the obligation of the administration to give reasons for its decisions.

Article 111 – Right to protection from damage
All shall have the right to require the United Federation of the World to make good any damage caused by its institutions or by its servants in the performance of their duties, in accordance with the general principles common to the laws of the Member States.

Article 112 – Right to write to institutions
All shall have the right to write to the institutions of the United Federation of the World in one of the languages of the Constitution and must receive an answer in the same language.

Article 113 – Right of access to documents
All world citizens of the United Federation of the World and all persons or organisations residing in or having a registered office

in a Member State shall have a right of access to documents of the institutions, bodies, offices and agencies of the United Federation of the World.

Article 114 – Right to appeal to World Ombudsman
All world citizens of the United Federation of the World and all persons or organisations residing in or having a registered office in a Member State shall have the right to refer to the World Ombudsman cases of maladministration in the activities of the institutions, bodies, offices or agencies of the United Federation of the World, with the exception of the World Court of Justice or any World Tribunal of the United Federation of the World acting in its judicial role.

Article 115 – Right to petition
All world citizens of the United Federation of the World and all persons or organisations residing in or having a registered office in a Member State shall have the right to petition the World Parliamentary Assembly and the World Senate of the United Federation of the World.

Article 116 – Right to recognition of languages
All world citizens shall have an equal right to speak and write their language and to have their language recognised. Languages are the means of human communication, and the United Federation of the World shall recognise and protect all the languages spoken by world citizens in the Member States. It regards all languages as having equal status and as reflecting the diversity of civilizations, nations and races:

1. *Protection of endangered languages*
   The United Federation of the World shall protect endangered languages, which include all indigenous languages and the languages of linguistic minorities.

2. *Research into languages of ancient civilizations*
   The United Federation of the World shall encourage all world citizens to undertake research into the languages of ancient civilizations to perpetuate ancient knowledge and wisdom and a high civilization.

Article 117 – Six working languages
The United Federation of the World shall inherit the United Nations' tradition of six working languages: Arabic, Chinese, English, French, Russian and Spanish. These six working languages are based on the mother tongue or second language of almost three billion people, nearly half the world's population, and are official languages in more than half the Member States. The United Federation of the World shall seek to expand its working languages to promote peaceful communication and cross-cultural dialogue between Member States and world citizens.

Article 118 – Purpose of Constitution
With reference to Article 1 on the Purposes of the United Federation of the World, the purpose of this Constitution shall be to secure "the common good" of all world citizens.

Article 119 – Depositing of Constitution
This Constitution, whose Arabic, Chinese, English, French, Russian and Spanish texts are equally authentic, shall be deposited in the archives of the United Nations, which shall eventually be transformed into the archives of the United Federation of the World, where it can be accessed on the internet by all world citizens. (See also Article 140.)

CHAPTER X: PROTECTION OF RIGHTS AND FREEDOMS

Article 120 – Right to Protection by this Constitution
The fundamental rights and freedoms of all world citizens shall be protected by the Constitution of the United Federation of the World and the laws of its Member States.

Article 121 – Entitlement to a social and international order
All shall be entitled to a social and international order in which the rights and freedoms set out in this Constitution can be fully realised.

Article 122 – Respect for the rights and freedoms of others
In the exercise of rights and freedoms, all shall be required by law to recognise and respect the rights and freedoms of others.

Article 123 – Procedure of amendment protects rights and freedoms more extensively
This Constitution's procedure of amendment (see Chapter XIII) shall protect the fundamental rights and freedoms of world citizens more extensively.

Article 124 – Application of Constitution and respect for rights
The provisions of this Constitution shall apply to the institutions, bodies, offices and agencies of the Federation with due regard for the principle of subsidiarity and to the Member States only when they are implementing Federation law. They shall therefore respect the rights, observe the principles and promote the application of the provisions in accordance with their respective powers.

Article 125 – Scope and interpretation of rights in relation to precedents
In so far as this Constitution contains rights which correspond to rights guaranteed by precedents in the legal documents of *The Charter of the United Nations, The Universal Declaration of Human Rights, The International Covenant on Economic, Social and Cultural Rights, The International Covenant on Civil and Political Rights, The European Convention for the Protection of Human Rights and Fundamental Freedoms, The Charter of Fundamental Rights of the European Union* and of other precedents listed in Appendix 1A, and of international treaties and the constitutions of Member States, the meaning and scope of the Constitution's rights shall be the same as those laid down by these precedents. This provision shall not prevent Federation law from providing more extensive protection than the laws of these precedents.

Article 126 – Level of protection
Nothing in this Constitution shall be interpreted as restricting or adversely affecting human rights and fundamental freedoms as recognised, in their respective fields of application, by Federation law and international law, and by international agreements to which the United Federation of the World or all the Member States are party, and by the Member States' constitutions.

Article 127 – Preservation of world citizens' other rights
The enumeration in the Constitution of certain rights shall not be construed as denying or disparaging other rights retained by world citizens.

Article 128 – Prohibition of abuse of rights
Nothing in this Constitution shall be interpreted as implying for any Member State, group or person any right to engage in any activity or to perform any act aimed at the destruction of any of the rights and freedoms set out in this Constitution.

Article 129 – Powers reserved to Member States or world citizens
The powers not delegated to the United Federation of the World by this Constitution are reserved to the Member States, or to world citizens.

Article 130 – World Constitutional Court to interpret Constitution
The supreme authority on the interpretation of fundamental rights and freedoms of world citizens in this Constitution shall be the World Constitutional Court of the United Federation of the World.

CHAPTER XI: EMBLEM, FLAG, ANTHEM AND LOCATION

Article 131 – Emblem
The United Federation of the World's emblem shall be a circle showing the empty UN General Assembly in burnt orange with the letters 'UF' (standing for 'United Federation') within it, with the letter 'U' on the left side and the letter 'F' on the right side, superimposed on the globe of the world (as shown on the front cover of the first edition of *World Constitution: Constitution for the United Federation of the World*). The two circles together suggest a World State and the administrative headquarters of the World Parliamentary Assembly.

Article 132 – Flag
The flag of the United Federation of the World shall consist of an orange sun on a sky-blue background. At the centre of the orange sun shall be a miniature of the official burnt-orange-and-blue emblem of the United Federation of the World with the letter 'U' on the left side and the letter 'F' on the right side. From a distance the flag shall resemble an orange sun on a blue sky.

Article 133 – Anthem

The anthem of the United Federation of the World shall be the following six lines excerpted from Tennyson's 'Locksley Hall' (1842):

For I dipt into the future, far as human eye could see,
Saw the Vision of the world, and all the wonder that would be;
Till the war-drum throbbed no longer, and the battle-flags were
   furled
In the Parliament of man, the Federation of the world.
There the common sense of most shall hold a fretful realm in awe,
And the kindly earth shall slumber, lapt in universal law.

"Parliament of man" suggests the World Parliamentary Assembly and "Federation of the world" anticipates 'United Federation of the World'. The silencing of the war-drum evokes a vision of the main goal of the United Federation of the World: the abolition of war and the inauguration of an age of peace, freedom and unity under "universal law". (See also Preamble.) This anthem shall be set to stirring music. (The words would fit Beethoven's Ninth-Symphony accompaniment to Schiller's *'An die Freude'*, more widely known as 'Ode to Joy'.)

Article 134 – Locations

The locations of the institutions of the United Federation of the World shall be debated and decided during the Constitutional Convention to be held at the UN General Assembly. Initially the location of the supranational tier of the United Federation of the World shall be in the UN, and of the World Parliamentary Assembly in the UN General Assembly, and shall be chaired on a rotational basis until elections can be held.

CHAPTER XII: SUPREMACY OF CONSTITUTION

Article 135 – Constitution the supreme law
This Constitution, and the laws of the United Federation of the World which shall be made in pursuance of its Articles, and all treaties made, or which shall be made, under the authority of the United Federation of the World, shall be the supreme law of the territories of all the Member States of the United Federation of the World; and the judges in every Member State shall be bound by this supreme law, notwithstanding anything in this Constitution or the laws of any Member State to the contrary.

Article 136 – Constitution supported by senators and representatives
The senators of the World Senate and representatives of the World Parliamentary Assembly, and the members of all Member-State legislatures, and all executive and judicial officers both of the United Federation of the World and of the Member States, shall be bound by oath or affirmation to support this Constitution.

CHAPTER XIII: AMENDMENTS

Article 137 – Adoption and ratification of amendments
Amendments to this Constitution shall come into force for all Member States of the United Federation of the World when they have been adopted by a vote of two thirds of the representatives of the World Parliamentary Assembly and of the senators of the World Senate and any twelve members of the World Executive Council, and when they have been ratified in accordance with their respective constitutional processes by two thirds of the Member States of the United Federation of the World, including all the permanent members of the World Executive Council.

Article 138 – Reviewing this Constitution at a General Conference
A General Conference of the Member States of the United Federation of the World for the purpose of reviewing this Constitution may be held at a date and place to be fixed by a two-thirds vote of the representatives of the World Parliamentary Assembly and of the senators of the World Senate and by a vote of any twelve members of the World Executive Council. Each Member State of the United Federation of the World shall have one vote in the General Conference.

Article 139 – Alterations take effect on ratification
Any alteration of the present Constitution recommended by a two-thirds vote of the General Conference shall take effect when ratified in accordance with their respective constitutional processes by two thirds of the Member States of the United Federation of the World, including all the permanent members of the World Executive Council.

CHAPTER XIV: SIGNING AND RATIFICATION

Article 140 – Deposit of Constitution in the archives of the United Nations
This Constitution, of which the Arabic, Chinese, English, French, Russian, and Spanish texts are equally authentic, shall remain deposited in the archives of the United Nations, which shall eventually be transformed into the archives of the United Federation of the World. (See also Article 119.)

Article 141 – Ratifications of Constitution by signatory states
This Constitution shall be ratified by the signatory nation-states in accordance with their respective constitutional processes.

Article 142 – Deposits of ratifications in the archives of the United Nations
During the transitional period the ratifications shall be deposited in the archives of the United Nations, which shall notify all the signatory states of each deposit. The archives of the United Nations shall eventually be transformed into the archives of the United Federation of the World.

Article 143 – Constitution come into force and United Federation of the World comes into existence on deposits of key ratifications
This Constitution shall come into force, and the United Federation of the World shall come into existence upon the deposit of ratifications by the People's Republic of China, the French Republic, the Russian Federation, the United Kingdom of Great Britain and Northern Ireland, and the United States of America, and by a majority of the other signatory states. A protocol of the ratifications deposited shall be drawn up by the United Nations, which shall distribute copies of the ratifications to all the signatory states.

Article 144 – Signatory states become Member States on deposit of their ratifications
The states signing the present Constitution and ratifying it after it has come into force shall become Member States of the United Federation of the World on the date they deposit their ratifications in the archives of the United Nations.

Article 145 – Certified copies of deposits of ratifications to Member States
During the transitional period when the United Nations is still in existence, certified copies of the deposits of ratifications shall be distributed by the United Nations to the governments of the signatory states that are already Member States.

Signing of Constitution
IN FAITH WHEREOF the representatives of the Governments of the United Federation of the World have signed this Constitution. DONE at the Headquarters of the United Nations in the City of New York.

_____ Date

In witness whereof we have hereunto subscribed our names.

_____ Signatures

APPENDICES

Precedents and data on which the Constitution is based

Appendix 1

26 Constitutional Precedents and 204 Constitutions

(Many of the Articles in the Constitution were inspired by aspects of the precedents in A, see Sources for Articles in the Constitution for the United Federation of the World, p.81.)

A. 26 Constitutional Precedents consulted during the writing of *Constitution for the United Federation of the World*

1	Albany Plan of Union	10 July 1754
2	Declaration of Independence	4 July 1776
3	The Articles of Confederation	1 March 1781
4	The Federal Constitution	Signed/created 17 September 1787, ratified 21 June 1788
5	The Bill of Rights	15 December 1791
6	The Charter of the United Nations (The UN Charter)	26 June 1945
7	The UN Universal Declaration of Human Rights	10 December 1948
8	The North Atlantic Treaty	4 April 1949
9	Treaty of Paris	18 April 1951
10	European Convention on Human Rights (the Convention for the Protection of Human Rights and Fundamental Freedoms)	3 September 1953

11	Treaty of Rome	25 March 1957
12	Merger Treaty	8 April 1965
13	The International Covenant on Civil and Political Rights (ICCPR)	16 December 1966, 23 March 1976
14	The International Covenant on Economic, Social and Cultural Rights (ICESCR)	16 December 1966, 3 January 1976
15	Constitution for the Federation of Earth	1968, May1991
16	Schengen Agreement	14 June 1985
17	Single European Act	17 February 1986
18	Maastricht Treaty	7 February 1992
19	United Nations' Rio Declaration on Environment and Development	3–14 June 1992
20	Treaty of Amsterdam	2 October 1997
21	The Charter for Global Democracy	17 September 1999
22	The Charter of Fundamental Rights of the European Union (European Charter)	7 December 2000, 14 December 2007
23	Treaty of Nice	1 February 2003
24	Treaty establishing a Constitution for Europe (European Constitution)	2004 (rejected/unratified 2005)

| 25 | Treaty of Lisbon | 13 December 2007 |
| 26 | Constitution for the Universal State of the Earth | 7 October 2015 |

B. 186 Existing Constitutions

1. Constitutions of 158 Sovereign States

1	Afghanistan	4 January 2004
2	Albania	28 November 1998
3	Algeria	8 September 1963
4	Andorra	2 February 1993
5	Angola	21 January 2010
6	Argentina	1 May 1853
7	Armenia	5 July 1995
8	Australia	1 January 1901
9	Austria	1 October 1920
10	Azerbaijan	12 November 1995
11	Bangladesh	16 December 1972
12	Bahrain	14 February 2002
13	Barbados	30 November 1966

14	Belarus	15 March 1994
15	Belize	21 September 1981
16	Benin	2 December 1990
17	Belgium	7 February 1831
18	Bolivia	7 February 2009
19	Bosnia and Herzegovina	14 December 1995
20	Botswana	30 September 1966
21	Bhutan	18 July 2008
22	Brazil	5 October 1988
23	Bulgaria	12 July 1991
24	Burma	29 May 2008
25	Burundi	9 March 1992
26	Cameroon	18 January 1996
27	Canada	1 July 1867
28	Chad	31 March 1996
29	Chile	11 March 1981
30	China, People's Republic of	4 December 1982
31	Colombia	4 July 1991
32	Congo, Democratic Republic of	18 February 2006

33	Costa Rica	7 November 1949
34	Croatia	22 December 1990
35	Cuba	24 February 1976
36	Cyprus	16 August 1960
37	Czech Republic	16 December 1992
38	Denmark	5 June 1849
39	Dominican Republic	26 January 2010
40	Djibouti	15 September 1992
41	East Timor	20 May 2002
42	Ecuador	20 October 2008
43	El Salvador	20 December 1983
44	Egypt	18 January 2014
45	Equatorial Guinea	17 November 1991
46	Eritrea	23 May 1997
47	Estonia	28 June 1992
48	Ethiopia	21 August 1995
49	Fiji	6 September 2013
50	Finland	1 March 2000
51	France	4 October 1958

52	Gambia	16 January 1997
53	Georgia	24 August 1995
54	Germany, Federal Republic of, Basic Law	8 May 1949
55	Ghana	28 April 1992
56	Greece	11 June 1975
57	Guatemala	14 January 1986
58	Guyana	6 October 1980
59	Haiti	20 June 2012
60	Hungary	18 April 2011
61	Honduras	20 January 1982
62	Iceland	17 June 1944
63	India	26 January 1950
64	Indonesia	18 August 1945
65	Iran, Islamic Republic of	3 December 1979
66	Iraq	15 October 2005
67	Ireland	29 December 1937
68	Italy	22 December 1947
69	Ivory Coast	8 November 2016

70	Jamaica	1 January 1962
71	Japan	3 May 1947
72	Jordan	11 January 1952
73	Kazakhstan	30 August 1995
74	Kenya	27 August 2010
75	Kyrgyzstan	27 June 2010
76	Korea, Republic of	17 July 1948
77	Korea, Democratic People's Republic of, Socialist Constitution	25 December 1972
78	Kuwait	11 November 1962
79	Laos	14 August 1991
80	Latvia	7 November 1922
81	Lebanon	23 May 1926
82	Luxembourg	17 October 1868
83	Liberia	6 January 1986
84	Libyan Interim Constitutional Declaration	3 August 2011
85	Lithuania	25 October 1992
86	Liechtenstein	5 October 1921
87	Macedonia, Republic of	17 November 1991

88	Madagascar	14 November 2010
89	Malaysia, Federal Constitution of	27 August 1957
90	Maldives	7 August 2008
91	Mali	12 January 1992
92	Malta	21 September 1964
93	Mauritania	12 July 1991
94	Mauritius	12 March 1968
95	Mexico	5 February 1917
96	Micronesia, Federated States of	1 October 1978
97	Moldova	29 July 1994
98	Monaco	17 December 1962
99	Mongolia	13 January 1992
100	Montenegro	19 October 2007
101	Morocco	14 December 1962
102	Namibia	9 February 1990
103	Nauru	31 January 1968
104	Netherlands	29 March 1815
105	Nepal	20 September 2015
106	Nicaragua	1 January 1987

107	Niger	25 November 2010
108	Nigeria	29 May 1999
109	Norway, Kingdom of	17 May 1814
110	Oman, Basic Statute of	6 November 1996
111	Pakistan	14 August 1973
112	Paraguay	20 June 1992
113	Palestinian National Covenant	28 May 1964
114	Panama	11 October 1972
115	Papua New Guinea	16 September 1975
116	Peru	31 December 1993
117	Philippines	2 February 1987
118	Poland	2 April 1997
119	Portugal	25 April 1976
120	Romania	21 November 1991
121	Russia	12 December 1993
122	Rwanda	26 May 2003
123	Samoa	28 October 1960
124	Saint Kitts and Nevis	23 June 1983
125	Senegal	1 January 2001

126	Serbia	8 November 2006
127	Singapore	9 August 1965
128	Slovakia	1 October 1992
129	Slovenia	23 December 1991
130	Somalia	1 August 2012
131	South Africa	4 February 1997
132	South Sudan	9 July 2011
133	Spain	6 December 1978
134	Sri Lanka	7 September 1978
135	Sudan	9 July 2005
136	Suriname	30 September 1987
137	Sweden	1974, adopted 1 January 1975
138	Swiss Federal Constitution	18 April 1999
139	Syria	27 February 2012
140	Tajikistan	6 November 1994
141	Tanzania	25 April 1977
142	Thailand	6 April 2017
143	Tonga	4 November 1875

144	Tunisia	26 January 2014
145	Turkey	7 November 1982
146	Turkmenistan	18 May 1992
147	Uganda	8 October 1995
148	Ukraine	28 June 1996
149	United Arab Emirates	2 December 1971
150	United States of America	21 June 1788
151	Uruguay	15 February 1967
152	Uzbekistan	8 December 1992
153	Vanuatu	30 July 1980
154	Vatican City, Fundamental Law of State	26 November 2000
155	Venezuela	20 December 1999
156	Vietnam, Socialist Republic of	28 November 2013
157	Yemen	16 May 1991
158	Zimbabwe	9 May 2013

2. Constitutions of 9 Partially-Recognised Countries

1	Abkhazia	3 October 1999

2	China, Republic of (Taiwan)	25 December 1947
3	Kosovo	15 June 2008
4	Nagorno-Karabakh	10 December 2006
5	Northern Cyprus	5 May 1985
6	Sahrawi Arab Democratic Republic	August 1976
7	Somaliland	31 May 2001
8	South Ossetia	8 April 2001
9	Transnistria	17 January 1996

3. Constitutions of 13 Dependent Territories

1	American Samoa	17 October 1960
2	Aruba	1 January 1986
3	British Virgin Islands	15 June 2007
4	Curaçao	10 October 2010
5	Falkland Islands	1 January 2009
6	Gibraltar	2 January 2007
7	Hong Kong Basic Law	4 April 1990
8	Macau Basic Law	20 December 1999

9	Niue Constitution Act	19 October 1974
10	Northern Mariana Islands Commonwealth Constitution	1 January 1978
11	Puerto Rico	25 July 1952
12	Sint Maarten	10 October 2010
13	Turks and Caicos Islands	15 October 2012

4. 6 Uncodified Constitutions

1	Canada	
2	Israel, Basic Laws of	
3	New Zealand	
4	San Marino	
5	Saudi Arabia, Basic Law of (although the Basic Law also declares the Koran to be the Constitution of Saudi Arabia)	
6	United Kingdom	

C. 18 Constitutions of Former Countries

| 1 | Catalonia | 1413/1495 |
| 2 | Confederate States of America | 1861/1862 |

3	Corsica	1755
4	Czechoslovakia	1920, 1948, 1960, 1968
5	East Germany	1949, 1968, 1974, 1989
6	Hawai'i, Kingdom of	1840, 1852, 1887
7	Irish Free State	1922
8	Ottoman Empire	1876
9	Poland, Kingdom of	1815
10	Poland-Lithuania	1791
11	Prussia	1848, 1849, 1850, 1920
12	Russian Empire	1832, 1906
13	Serbia and Montenegro, Constitutional Charter of	2003
14	Soviet Union (USSR)	1924, 1936, 1977
15	Texas, Republic of	1836
16	Vermont Republic	1793
17	Weimar Republic	1919
18	Yugoslavia	1946

Appendix 2

World Parliamentary Assembly, Allocation of 850 Seats

This allocation takes account of, and adjusts for, national and territorial arrangements, countries' populations, nuclear influence and Permanent Membership of the UN Security Council. (For detailed thinking behind this allocation, see *World State*, pp.166–170.)

Letter relating to Appendix E3 in *World State*	Countries	No. each	Seats
A	The 4 largest countries: China, India, the EU (on the basis of 26 members all marked A, excluding the UK and France, see B), the US	30 each	120
B	3 Permanent Members of the Security Council: The Russian Federation, France, the UK	15 each	45
C	The 10 largest countries after the 4: Indonesia, Brazil, Pakistan, Nigeria, Bangladesh, Japan, Mexico, Ethiopia, Philippines, Egypt	12 each	120
D	The 15 next-largest countries: Vietnam, Democratic Republic of Congo, Iran, Turkey, Thailand, Tanzania, South Africa, Myanmar (Burma), South Korea, Colombia, Kenya, Argentina, Ukraine, Sudan, Uganda	8 each	120
E	The 20 next-largest countries: Algeria, Iraq, Canada, Morocco, Saudi Arabia, Uzbekistan, Malaysia, Peru, Venezuela, Nepal, Angola, Ghana, Yemen, Afghanistan, Mozambique, Australia, North Korea, Taiwan, Cameroon, Côte d'Ivoire	6 each	120

F	The 30 next-largest countries: Madagascar, Niger, Sri Lanka, Burkina Faso (formerly the Republic of Upper Volta), Syria, Mali, Malawi, Chile, Kazakhstan, Ecuador, Guatemala, Zambia, Cambodia, Senegal, Chad, Zimbabwe, Guinea, Republic of South Sudan (separated from Sudan in 2011), Rwanda, Tunisia, Cuba, Bolivia, Somalia, Haiti, Benin, Burundi, Dominican Republic, United Arab Emirates, Jordan, Azerbaijan	4 each	120
G	The 40 next-largest countries: Belarus, Honduras, Tajikistan, Israel, Switzerland, Papua New Guinea, Togo, Serbia, Sierra Leone, Paraguay, El Salvador, Laos, Libya, Nicaragua, Kyrgyzstan, Lebanon, Singapore, Eritrea, Norway, Central African Republic, Costa Rica, New Zealand, Turkmenistan, Republic of the Congo, Oman, Kuwait, Liberia, Panama, Mauritania, Georgia, Moldova, Bosnia and Herzegovina, Uruguay, Mongolia, Armenia, Albania, Jamaica, Qatar, Namibia, Botswana	3 each	120
H	The 48 next-largest countries: Republic of Macedonia, Lesotho, Gambia, Gabon, Guinea-Bissau, Bahrain, Trinidad and Tobago, Mauritius, Equatorial Guinea, East Timor, Swaziland, Djibouti, Fiji, Comoros (an island nation in the Indian Ocean), Bhutan, Guyana, Solomon Islands, Montenegro, Suriname, Cape Verde, Brunei, Belize, Bahamas, Maldives, Iceland, Northern Cyprus, Barbados, Vanuatu (an island nation in the South Pacific), Samoa, São Tomé and Principe (an island nation in the Gulf of Guinea), Saint Lucia, Kiribati (formerly known as the Gilbert Islands, in the Pacific Ocean), Saint Vincent and the	1 each	48

	Grenadines, Grenada, Tonga, Federated States of Micronesia, Seychelles, Antigua and Barbuda, Andorra, Dominica, Marshall Islands, Saint Kitts and Nevis, Liechtenstein, Monaco, San Marino, Palau (an island nation in the Pacific Ocean), Tuvalu (formerly known as the Ellice Islands, in the Pacific Ocean), Nauru (formerly known as Pleasant Island, in the South Pacific)		
I	2 non-UN-members with largest populations: Palestine, Puerto Rico	1 each	2
	Initial total		815
J	26 dependent territories outside the UN and not yet independent with associate status until they become independent, seats held in reserve for when they become independent: Macau, Western Sahara, French Polynesia, New Caledonia, Guam, Curaçao (an autonomous region of the Netherlands in the Caribbean), Aruba (an autonomous region of the Netherlands in the Caribbean), US Virgin Islands, Jersey (UK), Isle of Man (UK), Guernsey (UK), Bermuda (UK), Cayman Islands (UK), American Samoa, Northern Mariana Islands (a commonwealth in political union with the US, in the Western Pacific), Greenland (Denmark), Faroe Islands (Denmark), St Maarten (Netherlands), Saint-Martin (France), Gibraltar (UK), Turks and Caicos Islands (UK), British Virgin Islands (UK), Bonaire (an autonomous region of the Netherlands in the Caribbean), Cook Islands (New Zealand), Anguilla (UK), Vatican City (in view of its diplomatic importance)	1 each	26

K	9 disputed territories not on the UN-based list: Indian Kashmir (Jammu and Kashmir), Tibet, Pakistani Kashmir (Azad Kashmir), Kosovo, Chechnya, Transnistria, Abkhazia, Nagorno-Karabakh, South Ossetia	1 each	9
L	13 island groups with populations under 12,000 to be represented by colonial power: Wallis and Futuna (France), St Barthélemy (France), Saint Pierre and Miquelon (France), Saint Helena, Ascension and Tristan da Cunha (UK), Montserrat (UK), Sint Eustatius (Netherlands), Falkland Islands (UK), Norfolk Island (Australia), Christmas Island (Australia), Saba (Netherlands), Niue (New Zealand), Tokelau (New Zealand), Cocos (Keeling) Islands (Australia), Pitcairn Islands (UK)		0
	Eventual total		850

Appendix 3

World Commission, Allocation of 27 Seats

This allocation takes account of regional representation, population percentages, topographical extent, Permanent Membership of the UN Security Council, and possession of nuclear warheads to be disarmed. The reasons for the allocation are summarised in brackets. The abbreviation R means that there are regional considerations for the nomination; PM means Permanent Member of the UN Security Council; N means that there are nuclear/disarmament considerations behind the nomination; and wpp means world population percentage. The number 1 means one member to be nominated by a particular nation-state. Thus 1 China means one member nominated by China. (For more detailed thinking behind this allocation, see *World State*, pp.176–177.)

1   China (PM, N, wpp 18.5%)

1   Communist Asia (Mongolia, North Korea, N, Laos, Vietnam)

1   Russian Federation (PM, N, largest country in world)

1   Central Asia (ex-USSR)

1   Canada (topographical size) and Greenland

1   USA (PM, N)

1   UK (PM, N)

1   France (PM, N)

1   Western Europe including Germany (R)

1   Eastern Europe (R)

1   Central America and Caribbean (R)

1   North-East South America (including Brazil, N, R)

1   South-West South America (including Argentina, R)

1   Northern Africa (R)

1   Southern Africa (R)

1   Arab Middle East (R)

1   Israel (N)

1   Iran (N?)

1   Pakistan (N)/Afghanistan (R)

1   India (N, wpp 17.9%)

1	West-Central and South-East Asia (Bangladesh to Cambodia, R)
1	East Asia (Japan, South/North Korea, Philippines, R)
1	Indonesia (wpp 3.5%)/Malaysia
1	Australia/Oceania (R, wpp 0.5%)
1	UN (secondment of executive expert)
1	World Bank (secondment of expert)
<u>1</u>	Agencies of global government (secondment of expert)
27	Total

Appendix 4

World Senate, Allocation of 92 Seats

This allocation takes account of regional representation, population percentages, topographical area, possession of nuclear weapons to be disarmed, political clout and environmental considerations. The numbers below refer to the 46 zonal regions or constituencies, each of which elects 2 senators, total 92 seats. (For the detailed thinking behind this allocation, see *World State*, pp.179–180.)

4   China: East, West, North (including Mongolia), South (PM, N, wpp 18.5%)

3   Russian Federation: East, Central, West (PM, N)

2   Central Asia: North-Central (including Kazakhstan), South-Central (including Pakistan)

3   Canada: East, West, North (including Greenland and Arctic)

4   USA: East, West, North, South, including dependent territories (PM, N)

1   UK (PM, N)

1   France (PM, N)

4   Europe: 2 North-Western (including Scandinavia, Germany), 1 Eastern, 1 Southern (i.e. Northern Mediterranean – Spain, Italy, Greece/Aegean)

1   Central America, including Mexico

1   Caribbean

3   South America: North-East (Brazil, Bolivia, Paraguay), South (Argentina, Chile, Uruguay and Antarctica), North-West (Peru, Ecuador, Colombia, Venezuela, North Coast)

4   Africa: North, East, West (including Atlantic Ocean), South (NB Middle Africa distributed among these 4)

2   Middle East: Northern (including Turkey, Iraq), Southern (including Egypt, Saudi Arabia)

1   Israel

1   Iran

3   India, North (including Nepal), Central, South (including

Sri Lanka, Maldives and Indian Ocean)

2 East-Central Asia (Bangladesh, Myanmar/Burma, Thailand, Laos, Vietnam, Cambodia)

1 South-East Asia (Malaysia, Indonesia, wpp 3.9%)

2 East Asia (Japan, North/South Korea, Philippines)

2 Australia: East, West

<u>1</u> Oceania (New Zealand, islands and dependent territories)

46 Total

Appendix 5

Diagram/Flow Chart of the Supranational Authority:
The Structure of the World State

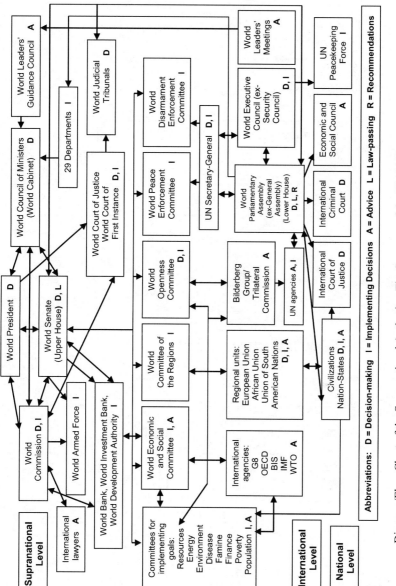

Diagram/Flow Chart of the Supranational Authority: The Structure of the World State

Appendix 6

Chart of 25 Civilizations and Cultures from One to One

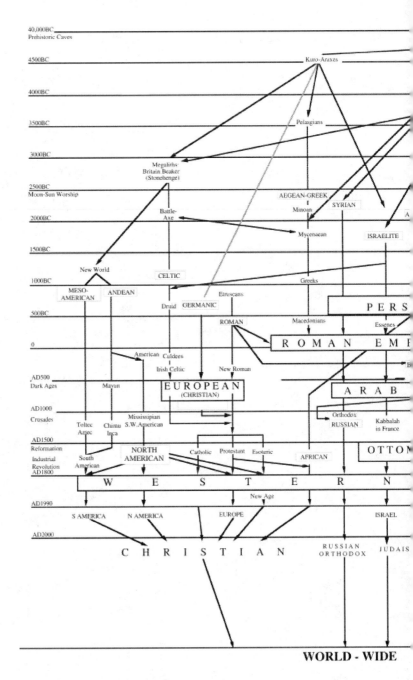

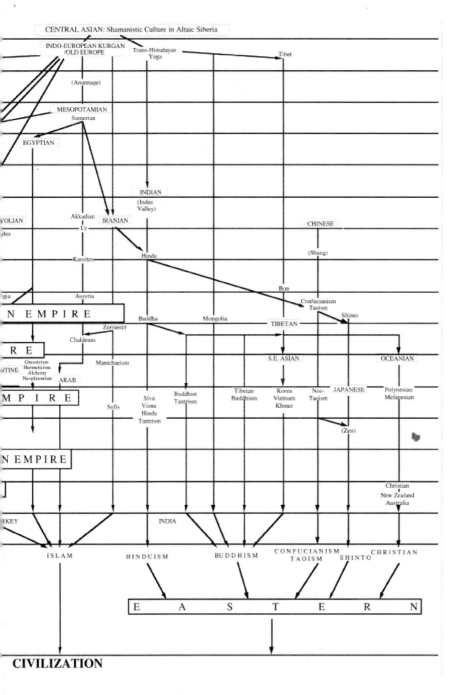

CENTRAL ASIAN: Shamanistic Culture in Altaic Siberia

INDO-EUROPEAN KURGAN /OLD EUROPE   Trans-Himalayan Yoga   Tibet

(Anunnage)

MESOPOTAMIAN
Sumerian

EGYPTIAN

INDIAN
(Indus Valley)

'OLIAN
ites   Akkadian   IRANIAN   CHINESE
Ur

Kassites   Hindu   (Shang)

Bon

gia   Assyria   Confucianism Taoism

N   E M P I R E   Buddha   Mongolia   Shinto
Zoroaster   TIBETAN

R E   Chaldeans

S.E. ASIAN   OCEANIAN

NTINE   Gnosticism Hermeticism Alchemy Neoplatonism   Manichaeism
ARAB

M P I R E   Buddhist Tantrism   Tibetan Buddhism   Korea Vietnam Khmer   Neo-Taoism   JAPANESE   Polynesian Melanesian
Sufis   Siva Visnu Hindu Tantrism

(Zen)

N EMPIRE

Christian New Zealand Australia

KEY   INDIA

ISLAM   HINDUISM   BUDDHISM   CONFUCIANISM TAOISM   SHINTO   CHRISTIAN

E   A   S   T   E   R   N

CIVILIZATION

Sources for Articles in the
Constitution for the United Federation of the World

Articles based on Nicholas Hagger's works and adapted precedents
Nicholas Hagger (NH) was preparing to write a constitution for a new World State from at least 2006, before he began writing *The New Philosophy of Universalism* (2009). (See p.xii.) He included precedents in the Appendices of three of his books, the first of which came out in 2007 (see p.84).

Below are the sources he drew on when writing and compiling the Articles for each Chapter: excerpts from his own works and Articles in some of the 26 precedents he consulted (see Appendix 1A). "Loosely based on/ influenced by" (below) means that he had a particular precedent in mind when he adapted it into an Article in this Constitution. (Precedents are rooted in a different time and have to be adapted to the circumstances of our contemporary world. For example, the purposes and principles of the UN Charter, which were shaped by the circumstances of 1945, are very different from, and have to be adapted to reflect, the purposes and principles of a contemporary World State.) It must be stressed that most of the Articles are based on excerpts from NH's works and are therefore in his own words.

Works by NH referred to in the sources below are abbreviated as follows:

SFA, The Secret Founding of America (2007)
WG, The World Government (2010)
SADr, The Secret American Dream (2011)
SADe, The Secret American Destiny (2016)
DoE, The Dream of Europa (2015)
PfoT, Peace for our Time (2018)
WS, World State (2018)

Sources for the 145 Articles of the Constitution for the United Federation of the World

PREAMBLE
Preamble by NH, first line loosely based on/influenced by the Federal Constitution, 1787 (in *SADr*, pp.253–266).

CHAPTER I: PURPOSES AND PRINCIPLES
Articles 1–2 by NH, loosely based on/influenced by Chapter I of the UN Charter, 1945.

CHAPTER II: MEMBERSHIP
Articles 3–6 by NH, loosely based on/influenced by Chapter II of the UN Charter, 1945. Same considerations addressed in different context. The suspension of rights and privileges in Article 5 shall be less drastic than the punitive sanctions in Article 6.

CHAPTER III: STRUCTURE
Article 7 by NH.
Article 8 by NH, based on *WS*, p.189 (and many other references to political Universalism in NH's works).
Articles 9–10 by NH, based on *WG*, pp.95–117; *SADr*, pp.193–199; *SADe*, pp.230–234; and *WS*, pp.165–187.
Article 11 by NH, based on NH's *WG*, pp.73–74; *SADr*, p.191; *SADe*, p.230; and *WS*, pp.105–106, 153, 195–196.
Articles 12–14 by NH, based on NH's *WG*, pp.95–117; *SADr*, pp.193–199; *SADe*, pp.230–234; *WS*, pp.165–187; and loosely based on/influenced by Chapter III of the UN Charter, 1945.
Articles 15–16 by NH, based on NH's *WG*, pp.95–117; *SADr*, pp.193–199; *SADe*, pp.230–234; and *WS*, pp.165–187.

CHAPTER IV: THE INTER-NATIONAL LEVEL
Articles 17–18 by NH, based on NH's *WG*, pp.95–117; *SADr*, pp.193–199; *SADe*, pp.230–234; and *WS*, pp.165–174.
Articles 19–21 by NH, based on NH's *WG*, pp.95–117; *SADr*, pp.193–199; *SADe*, pp.230–234; *WS*, pp. 165–174; and loosely based on/influenced

by Chapter IV of the UN Charter, 1945.

Article 22 by NH, based on NH's *WG*, pp.95–117; *SADr*, pp.193–199; *SADe*, pp.230–234; and *WS*, pp.165–174.

Articles 23–24 by NH, based on NH's *WG*, pp.95–117; *SADr*, pp.193–199; *SADe*, pp.230–234; *WS*, pp.165–174; and loosely based on/influenced by Chapter V of the UN Charter, 1945.

Articles 25–26 by NH, based on NH's *WG*, pp.95–117; *SADr*, pp.193–199; *SADe*, pp.230–234; and *WS*, pp.165–174.

CHAPTER V: THE SUPRANATIONAL LEVEL

Articles 27–45 by NH, based on NH's *WG*, pp.95–117; *SADr*, pp.193–199; *SADe*, pp.230–234; and *WS*, pp.174–187.

CHAPTER VI: PEACE DIVIDEND

Articles 46–47 by NH, based on NH's *WG*, pp.156–157, 164–165; *SADr*, p.200; *SADe*, p.234; *WS*, pp.190–192, 199–200.

Articles 48–50 by NH, based on NH's *WG*, pp.154–155, 164–165; *SADr*, pp.202–204; *SADe*, p.235; *WS*, pp.188–189, 207, 210.

Article 51 by NH, based on NH's *WG*, p.16; *SADr*, pp.219–220; *SADe*, p.243–244; and *WS*, p.20.

CHAPTER VII: RIGHTS AND FREEDOMS

Articles 52–86 by NH and loosely based on/influenced by the European Convention on Human Rights, 1948 (in *DoE*, pp.95–102); the UN Universal Declaration of Human Rights, 1953 (in *WG*, pp.203–210); and the Charter of Fundamental Rights of the European Union/European Charter, 2000, 2007 (in *DoE*, pp.103–117).

CHAPTER VIII: EQUAL RIGHTS AND JUSTICE

Articles 87–101 by NH and loosely based on/influenced by the European Convention on Human Rights, 1948 (in *DoE*, pp.95–102); the UN Universal Declaration of Human Rights, 1953 (in *WG*, pp.203–210); and the Charter of Fundamental Rights of the European Union/European Charter, 2000, 2007 (in *DoE*, pp.103–117).

CHAPTER IX: WORLD CITIZENS' RIGHTS

Articles 102–119 by NH and loosely based on/influenced by the Charter of Fundamental Rights of the European Union/European Charter, 2000, 2007 (in *DoE*, pp.103–117).

CHAPTER X: PROTECTION OF RIGHTS AND FREEDOMS

Articles 120–130 by NH and loosely based on/influenced by the Charter of Fundamental Rights of the European Union/European Charter, 2000, 2007 (in *DoE*, pp.103–117).

CHAPTER XI: EMBLEM, FLAG, ANTHEM, LOCATION

Articles 131–132 by NH, emblem shown on the front cover of *WS* and this book.

Article 133 by NH and lines from Tennyson's 'Locksley Hall' (1842).

Article 134 by NH, based on NH's *WG*, pp.155–156; *SADr*, pp.197–198; *SADe*, p.234; and *WS*, pp.189–190.

CHAPTER XII: SUPREMACY OF CONSTITUTION

Articles 135–136 by NH and loosely based on/influenced by Article VI, paragraph 2 of the Federal Constitution, 1787 (in *SADr*, pp.253–266).

CHAPTER XIII: AMENDMENTS

Articles 137–139 by NH and loosely based on/influenced by Chapter XVIII of the UN Charter, 1945.

CHAPTER XIV: SIGNING AND RATIFICATION

Articles 140–145 by NH and loosely based on/influenced by Chapter XIX of the UN Charter, 1945; and the last line of Article VII of the Federal Constitution, 1787 (in *SADr*, pp.253–266).

APPENDICES

Appendix 1: 26 Constitutional Precedents and 204 Constitutions.

All the constitutional precedents used in this Constitution except for the UN Charter can be found in Appendices in NH's *SFoA*, *WG* and *DoE*. The 26 constitutional precedents in A. were the main precedents consulted. Many of the remaining 204 constitutions in B. and C. can be found online.

Appendix 2: World Parliamentary Assembly, Allocation of 850 Seats. By NH, based on *WS*, pp.166–170.

Appendix 3: World Commission, Allocation of 27 Seats. By NH, based on *WS*, pp.176–177.

Appendix 4: World Senate, Allocation of 92 Seats. By NH, based on *WS*, pp.179–180.

Appendix 5: Diagram/Flow Chart of the Supranational Authority: The Structure of the World State. By NH, based on *WS*, p.173.

Appendix 6: Chart of 25 Civilizations and Cultures from One to One. By NH, based on *WS*, pp.216–217.

Bibliography

Works by Nicholas Hagger consulted during the writing of
Constitution for the United Federation of the World

Hagger, Nicholas, *The Dream of Europa*, O-Books, 2015.

Hagger, Nicholas, *The Fire and the Stones*, Element, 1991.

Hagger, Nicholas, *The Light of Civilization*, O-Books, 2006.

Hagger, Nicholas, *The New Philosophy of Universalism*, O-Books, 2009.

Hagger, Nicholas, *The Rise and Fall of Civilizations*, O-Books, 2008.

Hagger, Nicholas, *The Secret American Destiny*, Watkins, 2016.

Hagger, Nicholas, *The Secret American Dream*, Watkins, 2011.

Hagger, Nicholas, *The Secret Founding of America*, Watkins, 2007.

Hagger, Nicholas, *The World Government*, O-Books, 2010.

Hagger, Nicholas, *World State*, O-Books, 2018.

BOOKS

O-BOOKS

O is a symbol of the world, of oneness and unity; this eye represents knowledge and insight.